Antoni GAUDI

H KLICZKOWSKI

Idea and concept: **Paco Asensio & Hugo Kliczkowski**

Translation: **Books Factory *Translations***

Art director: **Mireia Casanovas Soley**

Graphic Design: **Emma Termes Parera**

Layout: **Soti Mas-Bagà**

Copy editing: **Raquel Vicente Durán**

La Fundición, 15. Polígono Industrial Santa Ana
28529 Rivas-Vaciamadrid. Madrid
Tel.: +34 91 666 50 01
Fax: +34 91 301 26 83
onlybook@onlybook.com
www.onlybook.com

ISBN: 84-96241-53-X
D.L.: B-42320-03

Editorial Project

LOFT Publications
Via Laietana, 32 4º Of. 92
08003 Barcelona. Spain
Tel.: 0034 932 688 088
Fax: 0034 932 687 073
e-mail: loft@loftpublications.com
www.loftpublications.com

Printed by:
Anman Gràfiques del Vallès, Spain

October 2003

Antoni Gaudi grew up in the rural Tarragona countryside, which is a rocky region replete with vineyards, olive and carob trees. The sharp observation of nature in his childhood lead him to his own individual conception of the world. Nature, with all of its wildlife and plants, contained all the building and structural laws that were needed in architecture for designing great edifices.

Whatever shortcomings in inspiration to be found in nature, Gaudí made up for them with his own ingeniousness. All Gaudí buildings are a reinterpretation of the canons followed in the creation of the universe, thus for Gaudí, the architect is akin to the Creator. Not surprisingly, such an iconoclastic outlook on architecture lead Gaudí to a life in which he only lived for his work, and his family life and the cultural and social life surrounding him, took a back seat.

Gaudí distrusted complex mathematical calculations but rather instead employed a simple

approach, careful observation of nature and empirical testing to resolve the problems that architecture posed. Consequently, he often realized countless experiments to calculate loads that a structure had to bear or the final shape that an ornament would take.

In the use of ceramics he was fortunate to receive the expertise of Manuel Vicens i Montaner, the renowned ceramic maker from Barcelona who commissioned him with the construction of a house. Elaborate work with wrought iron appears throughout the work of Gaudí as this industrial material takes on dynamic and exquisite shapes in the form of balconies, grates or lamps.

In the use of wood also, Gaudí shared inspiration with the artisans of his time, as he worked with them to elaborate some of his most imaginative designs. Finally, we need not neglect to mention his work with plaster, stone, brick and glass where he also collaborated very closely with the most highly qualified craftsman of his time.

Casa Vicens

***Construction date*: 1883-1888** ***Photographers*: Roger Casas, Pere Planells and Miquel Tres**

"When I went to take the measurements of the terrain, it was completely covered with tiny yellow flowers, which I adopted as my ornamental theme for the ceramics"

Carolines, 24-26. Barcelona

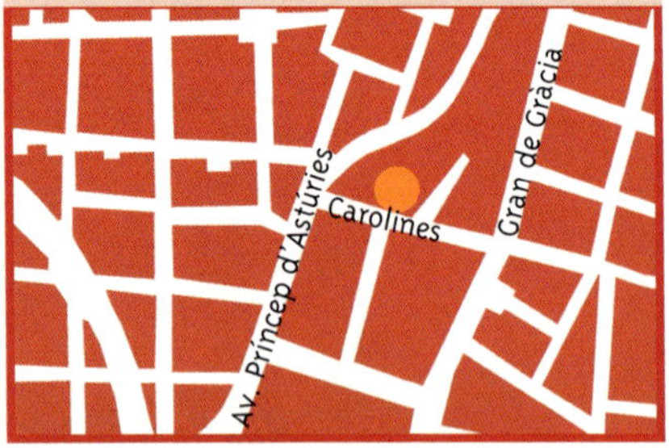

In 1883 the young Gaudí was faced with one of his first commissions as an architect. Although it is the work of a beginner, already we can denote the imagination, sensitivity and skill of the great artist. We can still perceive the straight lines that soon he would reject in favor of curves and impossible shapes. Without a doubt though, the "Gaudinian" seed is present in this ostentatious and singular construction.

Sited in the Gràcia neighborhood, Casa Vicens is a magnificent mixture of Spanish architectural forms of medieval inspiration, and includes important Arabic overtones more proper to Mudejar art than to building styles of the time.

The project called for a summer residence with a garden. Situated on a terrain of limited dimensions, it had to fit in with buildings of traditional design. These factors did not impede Gaudí from putting his own personal stamp on the work and create an unusual house perfectly adapted to its surroundings. He conceived a subtle combination of geometric volumes, which is masterfully resolved as he used horizontal strips on the lower part of the building and vertical lines. This is accentuated by the use of glazed ceramics as ornamentation on the upper part.

He chose simple materials for the exterior walls such as ocher-colored natural stone combined with brick.

Villa Quijano-El Capricho

***Construction date*: 1883-1885 *Photographer*: Pere Planells**

"The proprietor was called Díaz de Quijano and I said to myself: Quijano, Quijada... Quijote. It would be better not to go because we may have a hard time understanding each other"

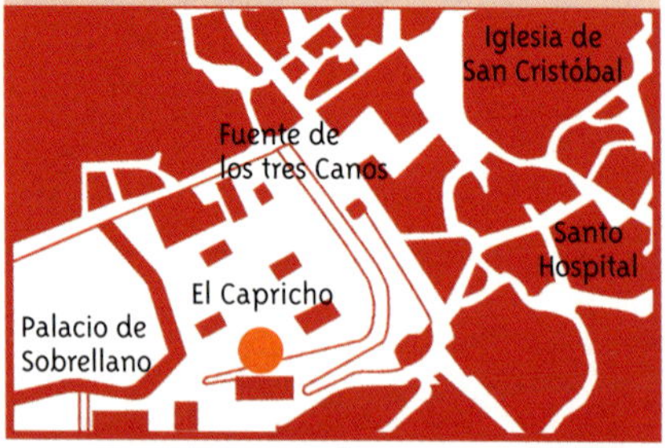

For the proprietor of this house, Máximo Díaz de Quijano, it was a caprice for him to have this residence in the country, which would suit his needs as a bachelor. For this reason Villa Quijano was nicknamed "El Capricho" (the caprice). Quijano commissioned the young Gaudí with the construction of the house, for which he did not see the plans, until it was finished.

It was built on the outskirts of Comillas, near Santander in the middle of the countryside. Similarities with Vicens House in Barcelona, which he was building at the same time, are quickly perceived. Resolved in a more restrained and austere way, there is a clear predominance of curved lines, which begin to take precedence over straight ones. Once again, the wish to combine forms proper to medieval Spanish architecture with those of Oriental reminiscence is evident.

Though imbued with his own original inspiration, he did not renounce functionality. Thus, the interior spatial arrangement is well adapted to the needs of the owner and it is outfitted with a slope roof, which adapts it well to the climatic conditions present there.

The compact building has a solid stone foundation. The homogeneity of the ocher and reddish-colored brick walls is broken by the lines of glazed ceramic, consisting of alternating sunflower and lush leaves in relief.

Finca Güell

***Construction date*: 1884-1887 *Photographer*: Pere Planells**

The gate of the dragon, with the dragon who guards over the "Gaudinian" universe that is hidden behind the gate, is a masterpiece of wrought iron inspired from Greek mythology

Eusebi Güell, one of Gaudí's best friends and one of his main patrons, commissioned him with the construction of an estate situated between Les Corts and Sarrià. Presently, they are neighborhoods in Barcelona but at the time they were towns on the outskirts of the city.

Apart from rehabilitating some already existing buildings, his task was to build other modules and additional elements: a wall with three gates to enclose the property, an elaborate main gate, a horse stable, a fountain, a lookout point, a chapel for the residence, and other diverse decorative complements.

The immense terrain has two entrance gates, one for pedestrians and one for carriages. It is flanked by two buildings, one with the caretaker's facilities, and the stable, which is connected to another building that is the riding school.

The caretaker's quarters consist of three volumes, a main octagonal-shaped one and two rectangular-shaped ones attached to it. The stable is one unitary rectangular space consisting of parabolic arches and covered vaults. Thanks to the use of trapezoidal openings, this area enjoys a generous amount of light, which is accentuated by the white color of the walls. Next to this pavilion is a small room with a quadrangular design and domed roof that is used as an exercise ring.

Between the caretaker's quarters and the stable is a large, wrought iron door that contains the sculpture of a dragon, which the workshop Vallet i Piqué handcrafted in 1885 from a design by Gaudí.

Avenida Pedralbes and avenida Joan XXIII

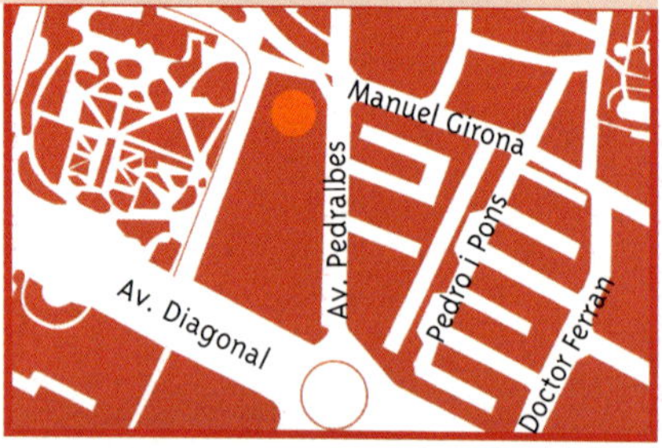

Sagrada Família

***Construction date*: 1883-1926 *Photographer*: Pere Planells and Miquel Tres**

"The temple of Sagrada Família will not be the last cathedral that is built but rather, may be the first in a new series of cathedrals"

Plaza de la Sagrada Família, Barcelona

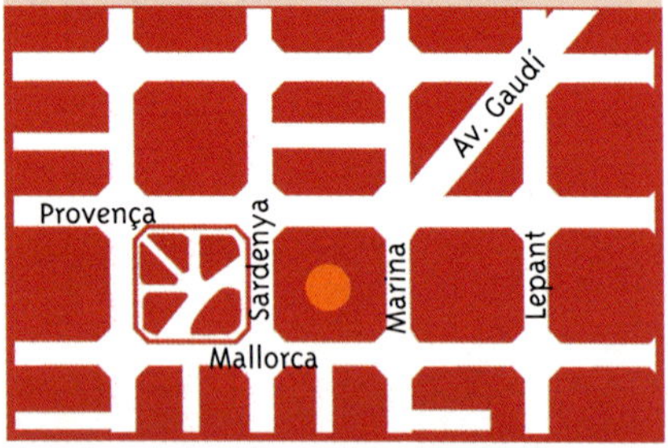

In 1887, the congregation of devotees of San José, led by the bookseller José María Bocabella, began the project of constructing a large temple financed with donations. The architect Francisco de Paula del Villar offered to draw up the plans for free. He designed a neo-Gothic church: three naves with a crypt oriented according to the site's orthogonal axis.

The first cornerstone was laid on March 19, 1882, the feast day of San José. Villar abandoned the directorship of the work one year later, after discrepancies with the committee over economic terms, since the project had already exceeded the provisions of the budget. Joan Martorell Montells, director of the committee, recommended that Gaudí, only 31 at the time, take charge of the construction. In 1884, Gaudí signed his first plans: the elevation and the section of the altar of the Chapel of San José, which was inaugurated one year later.

Unlike Villar's neo-Gothic project, Gaudí envisioned a church with numerous technical innovations and with a floor plan of the Latin cross placed on top of the initial crypt. Above it, the main altar was surrounded by seven chapels dedicated to the pains and sins of San José. The doors of the crossing are dedicated to the Passion and the Birth, and the principal façade, which opens onto Mallorca Street, to the Glory. Above each façade, Gaudí designed four towers, twelve in total, which represent the Apostles. Around the middle one, dedicated to Jesus Christ, there are four more dedicated to the evangelists and one to the Virgin.

Palau Güell

***Construction date*: 1886-1888 *Photographer*: Pere Planells**

For the singular dome in the interior of the building, conceived as a starry sky that presides over and floods the main hall with light, Gaudí received his inspiration from Saint Sofia

Nou de la Rambla 3-5, Barcelona

Declared a World Heritage building by Unesco, Palau Güell, another assignment that Eusebi Güell awarded to his protégé, is the building that permitted Gaudí to abandon anonymity. The architect designed this residence making use of all means available to him and without any budgetary constraints. For its construction he used the best stone, the best wrought iron and the best cabinetry, making this house the most expensive building of its time.

Due to the location of this urban palace, on a tight and narrow street in Barcelona's old quarter, it is impossible to take in a complete view of it from the exterior. Notwithstanding, Güell decided to establish his family residence there with two reasons in mind: to not abandon the family property there and to change the poor image of the neighborhood.

The sober and austere stone façade gives no clue to the majestic and opulent interior that Gaudí fashioned with unprecedented luxury. More than 25 designs preceded the definitive façade, which features portent historical lines and subtle, classical airs. Two large doors in the façade, in the form of parabolic arches, provide access for both carriages and pedestrians. The palace includes a basement, four floors and a terrace roof.

To reach the cellars, where there is a stable for horses, Gaudí created two ramps, one for the service and one for the horses. The first floor is located at street level and the principal staircase, which presides over the entrance, is placed between two halls.

Episcopal Palace in Astorga

***Construction date*: 1904-1906 *Photographer*: Roger Casas**

"In modern architecture, Gothic should be the starting point, but never the final destination"

Plaza Eduardo de Castro 24, Astorga, León

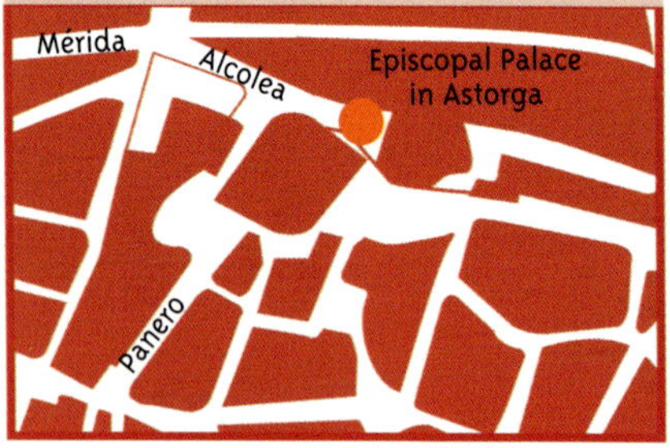

After a devastating fire completely destroyed the Episcopal Palace in Astorga, the Juan Bautista Grau i Vallespinós commissioned Gaudí to create a new Episcopal seat right next to the cathedral, on top of the wall. The relationship between the bishop and the architect was formed years earlier, when Grau was General Vicar of the Archdiocese of Tarragona. The bishop had inaugurated the chapel of the college of Jesus and Mary in Reus, where Gaudí had designed the alabaster altar and where his niece, Rosita Egea, had studied.

During the construction of the Astorga Palace, the two men had long conversations about liturgical reforms. Gaudí would later base his designs for the Sagrada Família on these. The first proposals that Gaudí sent delighted Grau, but they did not convince the architecture section of the Academy of San Fernando in Madrid, which oversaw all ecclesiastical projects. After various modifications, the committee approved Gaudí's project, even though there was a heated debate over his design. After Grau's death, Gaudí abandoned the Astorga project. A building, which brings to mind medieval fortifications and replete with Gothic elements, was erected.

The building was surrounded by a moat to facilitate ventilation and to illuminate the basement. The ground floor contains the kitchen, the secretary's office, the conference room, and the ecclesiastical courtroom. The first floor accommodates the library, the bishop's office, the chapel, and the guest rooms.

Theresian School

***Construction date*: 1888-1889 *Photographers*: Luis Gueilbuert and Roger Casas**

"The more time we spend reflecting on new ideas in architecture, the more convinced we are of the need to put them to use"

Ganduxer 85, Barcelona

Several conditions exerted a strong influence on the design of this "Teresiana" school located in the Sant Gervasi neighborhood in Barcelona. For one, the Carmelite community takes a vow of poverty. The building is also dedicated to the founder of the order of Saint Theresa, and adheres to a philosophy of life in agreement with the postulates of the Middle Ages.

Another architect oversaw the initial work of the site, including the beginning of the construction of a complex with three buildings. When Gaudí took over in March 1889, the first and second floors of the building had already been determined.

Gaudí stayed within the budget for the project, which was limited in comparison to the funds he had for other commissions. He also followed the guidelines put in place by the previous architect, which meant that certain stretches could not be modified. His design respected the austerity, asceticism and sobriety that this ecclesiastical order required without abandoning his original and imaginative style. Gaudí exercised restraint and designed a building with striking yet contained elements. This restraint was absent in his previous works but here it plays a starring role, at least in respect to the forms, as on closer observation we see that the building is full of symbolic elements.

For the exterior façade of this complex for the education of girls and nuns, Gaudí designed a rigorous volume of stone and brick, which includes some ornamental ceramic elements.

Casa Botines

***Construction date*: 1892-1893 *Photographer*: Roger Casas**

It was a challenge for Gaudí to create a neo-Gothic work in the center of León. His project surpassed all expectations, fit in well with its surroundings and respected the environment

While Gaudí was finishing the construction of the Episcopal Palace in Astorga, his friend and patron, Eusebi Güell recommended him for the construction of a house in the center of León. Simón Fernández and Mariano Andrés, the owners of a company that bought fabrics from Güell, commissioned Gaudí to build a residential building with a warehouse. The nickname of the house comes from the last name of the company's former owner, Joan Homs i Botinàs.

With Casa Botines the architect wanted to pay tribute to León's emblematic buildings. Therefore, he designed a building with a medieval air and numerous neo-Gothic characteristics. The building consists of four floors, a basement and attic. Gaudí chose an inclined roof and placed towers on the corners to reinforce the project's neo-Gothic feel. To ventilate and illuminate the basement, he created a moat around two of the façades, a strategy that he would repeat in the Sagrada Família.

Gaudí placed the owners' dwellings on the first floor. Each has its own entrance door as one has access on the side façade and the other on the back. The upper floors house rental flats and the lower floor contains the company offices. The main door is crowned by a wrought iron inscription with the name of the company, and by a great sculpture of Saint George. During the restoration of the building in 1950, workers discovered a lead tube under the sculpture containing the original plans signed by Gaudí, and press clipppings from the era.

Caja España

Bodegues Güell

***Construction date*: 1895 *Photographer*: Pere Planells**

The winery sits on a site that was meant to be the first project that Gaudí would design for Eusebi Güell. This was supposed to be a hunting lodge but it was never built

Carretera C-246, Garraf, Barcelona

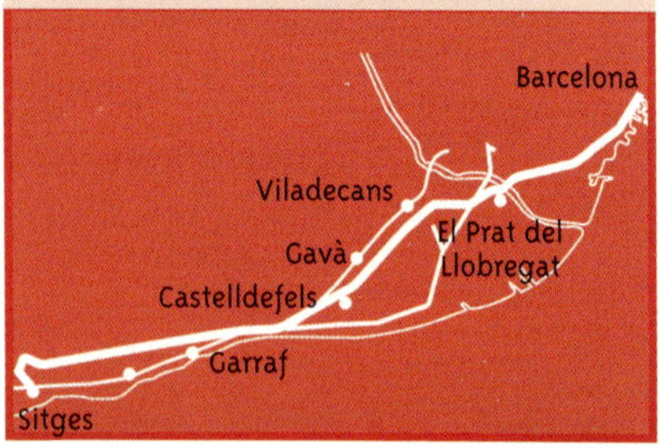

For many years, it was believed that the Bodegues Güell was designed by Francesc Berenguer i Mestres. However, the plans were not in the architect's archives and other factors led to the conclusion that Eusebi Güell had once again entrusted Gaudí to execute this project on one of his estates.

The land is located on the Garraf coast, to the south of Barcelona. At first, the client envisioned a hunting lodge, in a similar style to Casa Vicens. He later rejected the idea and decided instead to build a winery. Güell devoted the surrounding terrain to the cultivation of vineyards, which produced wine that was later served, for example, on the ships of the Transatlantic Company. The land was first leveled to even out the precipitous cliffs.

The development includes two buildings, the entrance pavilion and the winery. The front building has a large iron gate formed by a crossbeam of wrought iron with thick chains hanging from it. This combination of materials was not structurally necessary but Gaudí decorated some façades in this way in order to avoid simplicity. A grand arch crowned by a balcony with a superb view receives visitors and contains the door of the concierge's house.

The winery is located in an austere and striking building, evocative of military architecture and made of stone extracted from nearby quarries.

Crypt of the Colònia Güell

***Construction date*: 1908-1916 *Photographer*: Pere Planells**

"It is not a question of wishing to be original, because one's own style comes from within, and comes to the fore spontaneously"

The Colònia Güell is one of Gaudí's most original and interesting works, even though the project was never completed. Gaudí had free reign to design the project and spent almost 10 years in the elaboration of the plans. Construction began in 1908, but he was only able to build the crypt of the church. When Count Güell died in 1914, the project was abandoned.

The assignment entailed building a housing development for a small settlement of workers next to Eusebi Güell's textile factory in Santa Coloma de Cervelló, located 20 kilometers from Barcelona, in Baix Llobregat. Güell had planned to construct all types of facilities for the residents, including a church. An inspired Gaudí designed a complex ensemble with constant references to nature. For example, the church, situated on a small hill, would have blended in with its natural surroundings. Gaudí's plan was to use organic forms and a studied polychomy so that the dark tones of the bricks of the crypt would blend in with the tree trunks. The green tone of the church walls would blend in with the trees, and higher up, would change to blue and white in order to blend in with the sky and the clouds. For Gaudí, this special chromatic plan represented nature and symbolized, at a deeper level, the path of Christian life. His design took advantage of the land's pronounced slope to include a crypt with a portico and chapel.

Reixac s/n, Santa Coloma de Cervelló, Barcelona

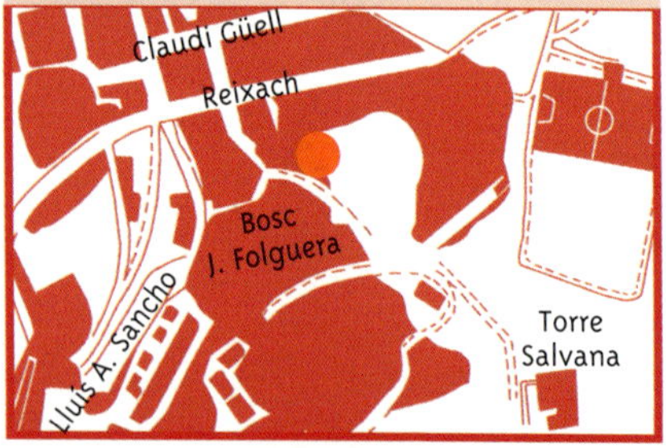

Bellesguard

***Construction date*: 1900-1909 *Photographers*: Miquel Tres and Joana Furió**

Bellesguard is Gaudí's greatest tribute to Catalonia's great medieval past

Bellesguard 16-20, Barcelona

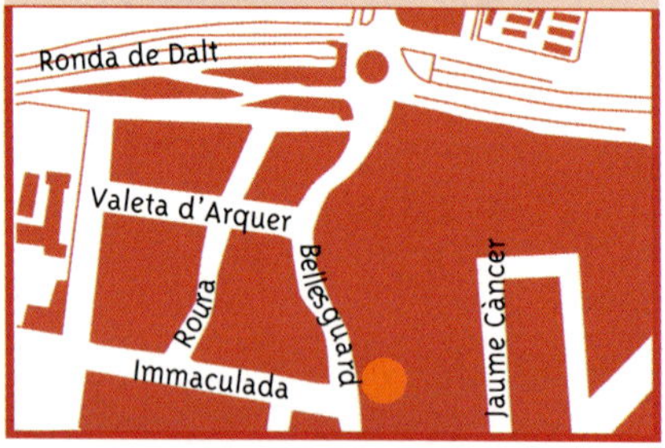

The country house of María Sagués, widow of Jaume Figueras and a fervent admirer of Gaudí, was constructed on land that, in the fifteenth century, was the site of the summer residence of the last Catalan-Aragonese king from the house of Barcelona, Martí I "the Human". In fact, the name of the estate, "Bellesguard" means beautiful view and dates from this era. It refers to the estate's striking location with a splendid view of the city of Barcelona.

When Gaudí accepted the commission to design María Sagués' home, few traces remained of what was formerly the king's medieval mansion. Gaudí respected the scant few ruins that remained. The volumes of the façades are endowed with Gaudí's personal style, as are the interiors replete with great architectural expressiveness.

The exterior of the building, covered with stone, is vaguely reminiscent of medieval constructions and adapts perfectly to its surroundings. The various windows that perforate the walls of the façade are lobed arches in the Gothic style. The tower situated at one of the extremes features one of the architect's most characteristic touches: the four-pointed cross.

Bellesguard is a residence with a simple, nearly square floor plan. The four principal diagonals are oriented towards the cardinal points. The house has a semi-basement, a ground floor, a floor above and an attic. Covered vaults with low profiles supported by cylindrical pillars define the structure of the semi-basement. On the upper level, the brick vaults are yet one more decorative element.

Park Güell

***Construction date*: 1900-1914** ***Photographers*: Pere Planells and Miquel Tres**

Gaudí's original idea was that of a residential city. With the passing of time however, it has become an urban park for all to delight in

Olot s/n, Barcelona

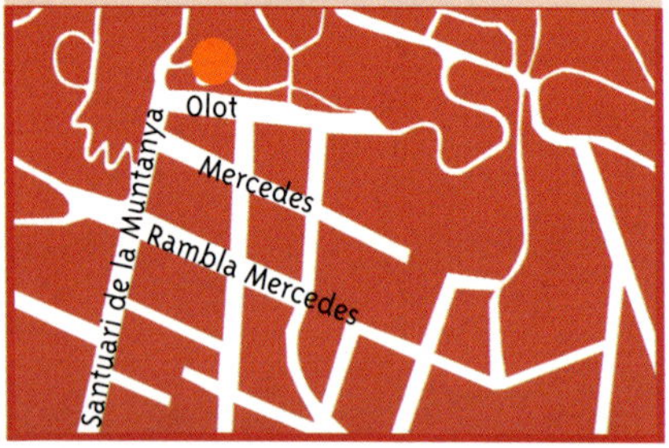

Eusebi Güell was an admirer of English landscape gardening. Envisioning a new model of the English "garden-city", he decided to develop some land known as the "Bald Mountain" in the neighborhood of Gracia. Güell entrusted the project to his friend and protégé Antoni Gaudí. His goal was to create a residential space close to the city that would attract the wealthy Catalan bourgeoisie. Unfortunately, the project was unsuccessful, and the terrain was converted into a public park in 1922, when Barcelona's City Hall bought the land from Güell's heirs.

Gaudí designed the complex as a housing development delimited with a surrounding wall. With seven gates, the wall features undulating lines and is made of masonry with ribbon-like trims with inlaid "trencadís", decorative compositions consisting of colorful broken ceramic pieces. This ornamentation is repeated in numerous compositional elements. The Park is divided into 60 plots. The tracts had a triangular form adapted to the topography of the land, full of uneven stretches and slopes. Only three of the tracts were sold. The Trias family bought two and Gaudí purchased the one used a display home, where he lived until he moved to the Sagrada Família. His former residence now houses the Gaudí museum.

Originally, the main entrance was situated on Olot Street. Two large medallions in the wall invite the visitor to come in. In one, in "trencadís" ceramic, is written "Park", and in the other, "Güell".

Finca Miralles

***Construction date*: 1901-1902 *Photographers*: Joana Furió and Roger Casas**

The undulating shape of the wall seems to come alive, as if a snake-like animal were the real guardian of the estate

Paseo Manuel Girona 55, Barcelona

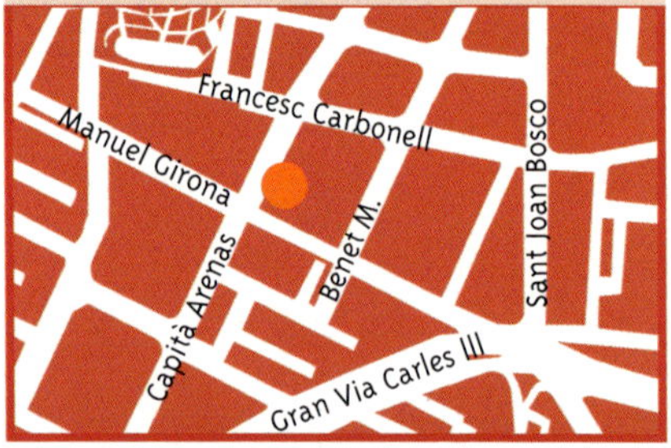

While Gaudí was immersed in his first grand residential project, Casa Calvet, he accepted another, smaller assignment. His friend Hermenegild Miralles Anglès asked him to design a gate and a surrounding wall for his estate on the road leading to the Finca Güell. Today, the road is a busy avenue between the neighborhoods of Les Corts and Sarrià. Even though some experts claim Gaudí drew the plans for the house and the small annex, which were later built on the estate by the architect Domènech Sugrañes, there is no evidence to support this.

The wall that Gaudí designed to surround the estate is wavy. Structurally, this meant that it needed more thickness in the base and a slimmer section in the upper part. For materials, Gaudí used ceramic bricks and the remains of Arabic tiles, together with lime mortar. He crowned the wall with an even continuous material that snakes along the top of it. The gate that he created for the carriages to enter through, has an irregular, arched form. The wall opens and folds to create access through a series of curves. A helical interior framework of variable thickness supports the door that seems to stand thanks to magic, since there is no external element that absorbs the eccentric loads. A marquee completes the wavy forms at the entrance. The marquee is formed by tie beams built into the door, and on which lie fiber cement tiles and helical braces.

Reformation of the Cathedral of Palma de Majorca

***Construction date*: 1903-1914 *Photographer*: Gabriel Vicens**

For Gaudí religion was not a passive activity, but rather, his boundless creativity inspired him to reinterpret liturgical spaces

Plaza Almoina, Palma de Mallorca

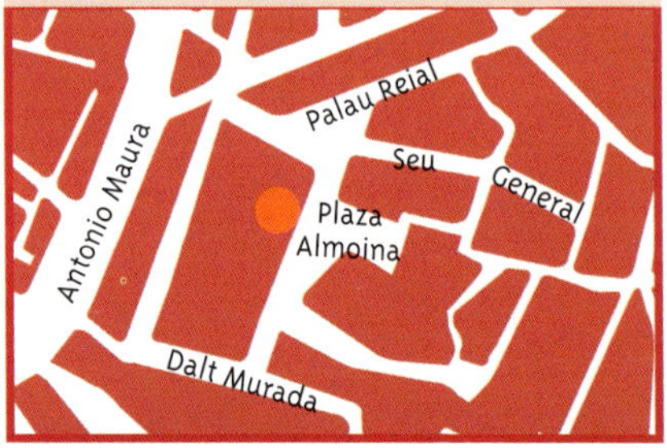

Bishop Pere Campins i Barceló met Gaudí in 1889, during the construction of the Sagrada Família. Campins was fascinated by Gaudís's artistic and architectural talent and was highly impressed by his knowledge of the Catholic liturgy, which the architect developed during his conversations with the bishop of Astorga. Years later the Cathedral Chapter approved Capins's proposal to restore the cathedral in Palma, which is regarded as one of the most beautiful examples of Catalan Gothic architecture. Without hesitation, the bishop assigned the project to Gaudí.

The architect's ambitious design aimed to emphasize the building's Gothic character. On one hand, Gaudí changed the site of some elements: he moved the choir of the nave to the presbytery and the small back choir to a side chapel. He also obtained permission to move the baroque altar in order to uncover and bring to the fore the old Gothic one. This left the Episcopal chair and the Trinidad chapel in full view. On the other hand, Gaudí designed new pieces to embellish and amplify the space, the most noteworthy being the railings, lights and liturgical furnishings. Having perceived a slight sagging of the columns, he also reinforced the structure by means of forged rings that also served as support for lights.

The relocation of elements made the altar the centerpiece, for which Gaudí designed an octagonal baldachin with symbolic references. The seven corners allude to the seven virtues of the Holy Spirit and the 50 small lamps are an allusion to the celebration of the Pentecost.

Casa Batlló

***Construction date*:** **1904-1906** ***Photographers*:** **Pere Planells, Joana Furió and Miquel Tres**

When the first rays of the morning light shine on the façade of Batlló House, it causes an iridescent effect and the first interplays of light

Passeig de Gràcia 43, Barcelona

Casa Batlló is located between Casa Ametller, designed by the modernist architect Puig i Cadalfalch, and a traditional building of the Eixample neighborhood, designed by Emili Sala. The building was constructed in 1877 and its owner, the textile manufacturer Josep Batlló i Casanovas, commissioned Gaudí to remodel the façade and to redistribute the inner courtyards. When Pere Milà, a friend of the industrialist, heard of Batlló's intention to renovate this house's image, he immediately presented him to Gaudí, of whom he was a fervent admirer. Even though the project meant working on an existing building, Gaudí imbued the project with his personal vision and Casa Batlló became one of the most emblematic projects of his extensive career.

The exterior of the building demonstrates Gaudí's compositional sensitivity. The first floors are covered with Marés sandstone and glass, while ceramic disks shroud the upper floors. During the renovation, the architect stood on the street and decided the optimal position of each piece so that they would stand out and afford optimal shine. The workers installed them one by one according to Gaudí's instructions. This manner of working —improving and perfecting an initial idea during the construction process— is repeated in all of Gaudí's works and reflects his dedication to his projects, which were almost never labeled, finished. This method caused some bureaucratic problems, since the authorities needed, and need, to approve finished projects.

Casa Milà

***Construction date*: 1906-1910** ***Photographers*: Joana Furió and Pere Planells**

"I would not be surprised if this building were converted into a hotel in the future, since it is so easy to change the distributions and there are so many bathrooms"

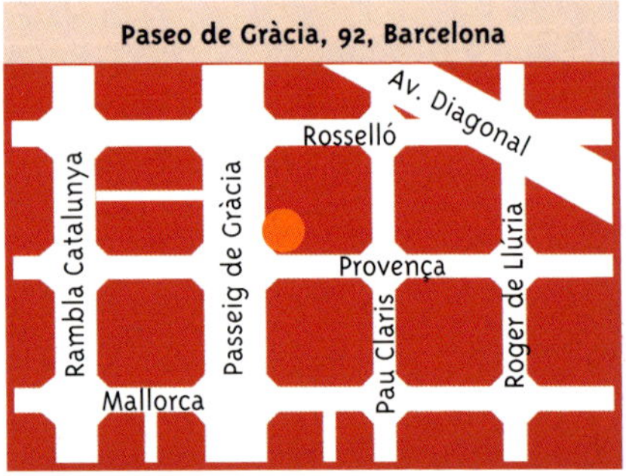

Casa Milà, located on one of the corners of the intersection of Passeig de Gràcia and Provença Street, rises up like a large, rocky formation. Ever since its construction, people from Barcelona have called it "La Pedrera" (the stone quarry). Pere Milà and his wife Roser Segimón charged Gaudí with its construction, and it was the architect's last civil project, since he later withdrew to work solely on Sagrada Família.

With this project, the artist wanted to make up for the lack of monuments in Barcelona, a lack of which he often denounced. His growing devotion to the Virgin Mary inspired a large building crowned by a bronze sculpture with the image of the Virgin, the patron of one of the proprietors, Roser Segimón. Even though in the end it was not crowned with the Virgin, La Pedrera still conserves some religious inscriptions.

Since it was a building of very large dimensions, Gaudí devised a system for saving on materials. He substituted load-bearing walls for a system of main beams and pillars. He carefully designed the links in order to reduce their section. He also fashioned a seemingly heavy façade. In reality, it is made up of slim, limestone plates from Garraf on the lower part, and plates from Vilafranca on the upper floors. The quantity of iron used has caused more than one expert in structures to tremble.

The sinuous forms of the façade, so often compared to the waves of the sea, have their counterpart in the interior. There, there are no right angles, fixed partition walls are nonexistent, and every detail is drawn to the millimeter.

Artigas Gardens

***Construction date*: 1905 *Photographer*: Miquel Tres**

Although Gaudí made use of resources similar to those used in Park Güell, here he included yet another element: water. Thus, he was able to create a fantastic, moist garden

La Pobla de Lillet, Lleida

After an extensive study conducted by the "Real Cátedra Gaudí", it was determined that Gaudí had in fact designed the gardens surrounding the old Artigas factory, in the province of Lleida. The architect received the assignment when he visited the prosperous industrialist, Joan Artigas i Alart, at his home in La Pobla de Lillet.

The estate is located on the banks of the Llobregat River, near its source. This presented the architect with the opportunity to design the only humid garden he would create during his career. The site is elongated and follows the course of the river. A bridge marks the natural entrance to the property and leads the visitor to a cave and a spectacular natural fountain called "La Magnésia", the name by which, in fact, the project is widely known.

A winding path leads to the second bridge where Gaudí intervened by building a small cylindrical arbor covered with a pointed dome, surrounded by walls made of stone. Further along the path, the visitor reaches the last bridge that Gaudí designed. The stones of this bridge are placed to resemble stalactites. One of the ends of the bridge becomes a pergola that both welcomes and shelters visitors from inclement weather.

In order to trace and embellish the route along the river, Gaudí also included numerous parterres and indigenous bushes. He erected small walls covered with little ceramic pieces, and placed various sculptures around the park.

Furniture

***Photography*: AZ Disseny SL**

Gaudí's renown mixture of styles, leaves his unmistakable personal touch, on all of his practically sculptural, pieces

Gaudí's imagination had no limits when it came to designing spaces and buildings. Nevertheless, his work was always characterized by a profound sense of rationalism and an in-depth knowledge of architectural norms. His contributions to the world of furniture design also featured this double virtue: functionality and originality.

Gaudí liked to be fully involved in every aspect of his projects. The pleasure of design inspired him to create furnishings and numerous decorative elements for both interiors and exteriors, including doors, peepholes, knobs, plant pots, grates and balconies.

His furniture designs featured solid forms and simple profiles. In a way, his pieces revived the lines of medieval furnishings, while displaying the lively, sinuous and zigzagging lines that are his trademark.

Created in a totally artisan manner, his furniture harmoniously combined ergonomics with beautiful and well-defined lines, often inspired by organic forms.

Others Minis by H Kliczkowski

La Fundición, 15 Polígono Industrial Santa Ana 28529 Rivas-Vaciamadrid Madrid
Tel. 34 91 666 50 01 Fax 34 91 301 26 83 asppan@asppan.com www.onlybook.com

Lofts
ISBN (GB) 84-96241-54-8

Minimalism. Architecture
ISBN (GB) 84-96241-58-0

Kitchens

Houses Design
ISBN (GB) 84-96241-57-2

Small Homes
ISBN (GB) 84-96241-55-6

Chill Out. Architecture & interiors
ISBN (GB) 84-96241-56-4

Gaudí step by step 1
ISBN (GB) 84-96241-50-5

Gaudí step by step 2
ISBN (GB) 84-96241-51-3

Gaudí step by step 3
ISBN (GB) 84-96241-52-1